POEMS

BY

MARIE TUDOR GARLAND

AUTHOR OF "THE POTTER'S CLAY,"
"THE WINGED SPIRIT," ETC.

(1917 — 1924)

PUBLIC DOMAIN POETS

Editor: Dick Whyte　　　　　—: No. IX :—　　　　　September 2022

MARIE TUDOR GARLAND (**1870-1945**) was the great grand-daughter of Judge William Tudor, State Senator and Secretary of the Commonwealth of Massachusetts, and granddaughter of Frederic Tudor, Boston's 'Ice King' and founder of the Tudor Ice Company. While from a conservative wealthy family, she was educated at Radcliffe, a liberal women's arts college, and local newspapers once described her as a "not so proper Bostonian." Tudor began publishing experimental 'free verse' in the 1910s, and was known for hosting "wild parties" at the Swan Lake Ranch in Santa Fe, attended by the likes of Georgia O'Keeffe and D.H. Lawrence. Painter and poet Kahlil Gibran also stayed with her in 1918, and reportedly had a 'glorious time'. She was also a committed feminist, and in 1920 attended the Eighth Congress of the International Women's Suffrage Alliance, writing that the event "seemed to hold more hope for the world than any international gathering in history." After the death of her first husband, Tudor married numerous times, and is said to have adopted more than 20 children over the course of her life.

A selection of verses from *The Potter's Clay* (The Knickerbocker Press, 1917), *The Winged Spirit* (G.P. Putnam's Sons, 1918), and *The Marriage Feast* (The Knickerbocker Press, 1920); with 'Autumn Mists' (*Rhythmus*, Jan. 1923) & 'The Desert' [excerpts] (*Poetry*, Oct. 1924). The introduction also quotes Tudor's article, 'Women's Internationalism' (*The Nation*, Aug. 1920).

Cover: Jan Poortenaar – 'Crane' & 'Rooster' (*The Apple*, April 1920). Inside: Donald Corley – 'The Fear of Being Afraid', 'The Woods of Westermain', 'The Dream House in the Wood' (*Rhythmus*, April-May 1923, etc.), & 'The Firmament' (*The Studio*, 1920); H. Gaudier-Brzeska – 'Elephant' (*The Apple*, etc.); 'Tree' (*Nassau Literary Magazine*, May 1921); 'Hooked Rugs in the Home of Marie T. Garland', in Elizabeth Waugh & Edith Foley, *Hooked Rugs* (The Century Co., 1927); 'With Hope...' (*The Winged Spirit*, 1918); 'Portrait' (*The Evening World*, March 1921), etc.

PUBLIC DOMAIN PRESS
Aotearoa / New Zealand
ISBN: 978-1-99-117763-6 (print) • 978-1-99-117765-0 (pdf)
978-1-99-117766-7 (kindle)

MARIE TUDOR GARLAND

SONGS FOR WOMEN & OTHER VERSES

I. THE POTTER'S CLAY
II. THE WINGED SPIRIT

A selection of verses from *The Potter's Clay* (1917)
& *The Winged Spirit* (1918).

III-VI. THE MARRIAGE FEAST

III. Marriage
IV. The Mother
V. The Woman
VI. Other Women

A selection of verses from *The Marriage Feast* (1920)
& two later poems (1923-4).

MARIE TUDOR GARLAND

POEMS
(1917 — 1924)

After man had conceived many gods
In his own image,
The woman said :
"The time has come
For me to conceive a god."
And the woman conceived,
And gave birth to herself.

Part I
The Potter's Clay

"I DID NOT THINK TO TOUCH THE SKY
WITH THESE TWO ARMS."

SAPPHO, 37.

UNTIL midnight Night will ride from Day,
Then will she hark toward the Dawn,
Riding fast—ever faster,
Until that moment of breathless passion,
When the two meet, and all the world is still—
As Night rides toward the Day,
So would I ride to you to-night in dreams.
Will you meet me in the dawn?

The Potter's Clay (1917)

"Five Long Shadows"

FIVE long shadows about the hill at sunrise,—
The fingers of Night clinging to the earth,
As it slipped beyond her grasp.

The Potter's Clay (1917)

WHEN dawn came
Fleecy clouds caught the sunrise,
Nature, dripping from last night's rain,
Sparkled in the sunlight.
   Everything in me hungered for life.

The sun is low,
Shadows from the trees beyond trail across the
     meadow,—
The closing of another day.
  And life is still beyond the hills.

MARKING the pulse of Time,
Love is but the beating of unborn wings ;
Upon the door of Life.

IF we pick up a stone and say,
"God's not in this,"
We bind the deity that way.

PASSION is the torch that guides us to the
    light,—
The music in our hearts,—our tears,
The pulse of time,
Our joy,—our pain.
It is the sunlight on the mountain,
The shadow in the vale,
Laughter rippling on the ocean,
The sob within the wave.

The Potter's Clay (1917)

"O Moon, Full Moon"

Moon, Full Moon,
I answer to your rune,—
Your ageless rune,
                    Of spring.
My thought an endless sea in flood,
A shimmering flood
                    Of spring.

The Potter's Clay (1917)

O Moon, Full Moon,
I crave of you a boon—
A boon
        Of spring.
In some form, wake me ever to the lure,
The ancient lure
        Of spring.

And Moon, Full Moon,
Let love be ever at its noon,
When I awaken—the timeless noon
        Of spring,
And make the waking sure,
As ever life is sure
        Of spring!

The Potter's Clay (1917)

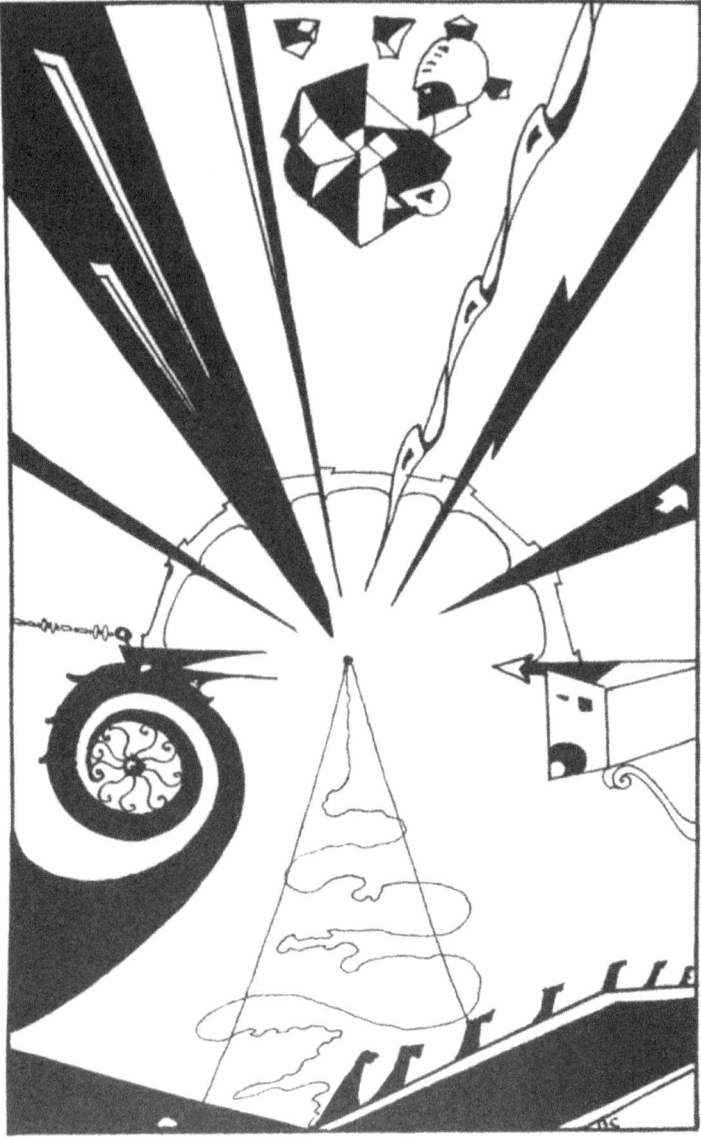

THE spirit has no resting place,
  Nor bides within a prison cell,
Except when self builds up the walls,
  Creating thus a self-made hell.

The Potter's Clay (1917)

My heart fares south to-night,
On wings of dream . . .
There, where the spring new-born
Is sweet with scent of earth
And fragrant flowers,
My spirit wanders,
And I dream. . . .

Soon the spring grown brave
Will northward creep to me,
With warm and tender hands
She'll feel her way along the hills,
Trailing, as she comes, her mantle green,
Wrought with jasmine and cherry bloom.

Her touch will wake the earth,
A thousand springs will live again in her—
A thousand springs in me make answer.

The Potter's Clay (1917)

OVER the surging sea of meadow,
Wind-tossed like spray,
Comes the song of the bobolink.

THE moon is full,
  Sea flooding,
  Sap flowing,
The moon is full,
  My thoughts winging,
  My man wooing,
The moon is full.

"Wood Thrush"

HARK, from the wood's melodious flute
That first clear liquid note,
Long sustained
Of summer!
You mean so much to me, shy hermit
Of the woods,
O messenger of joy!
From out your speckled throat
All music surely has its birth
In that clear, crystal note
Which bursts upon the ear,
Clearly calling, "Joy!—I'm here!"
Your first, full, rapturous note
Is like the colour in the crystal
When first the sun it catches,
With sparkling notes that follow
Dancing, in prismic flashes.

The Potter's Clay (1917)

First herald of the morning
In that long, liquid note of joy,
Buoyant, sportive, pealing,
The last to sing the closing note at vespers,
Plaintive, sweet, and full of depth
And feeling.

You fling your song out as a call,
You sing that in this life there's passion,
Pain and suffering—
But over all is joy!
      Joy!
         Joy!
There's joy enough for all!

The Potter's Clay (1917)

Part II

The Wingèd Spirit

TO MY LOVE

The bird must hunger
For his mate
Ere he will sing;
It is my love for you
That gives my spirit wings.

My heart is stilled at last to hold the joy of life,
As seas that catch the colours of the passing day.

The Winged Spirit (1918)

"Spirits"

WHY is it that, in all the wild tangle
Of Nature's garden, we become conscious
Of the throbbing of some wild spirits?
The sough and the sail, the moan in the pine
Tell of a mother's grief.   In the sunlight
Where the wind now wantons with the flowers,
We know the soul of the dead infant
Has won freedom and peace.

The Winged Spirit (1918)

"A March of Trees"

THE moon will lead a march of trees
To her theatre in the wood,
And watch their solemn pace,
In flank and column,
Around this magic place.

When a cloud slips past the moon
The last of the toiling column fades,
And night steals out,
To coil about
These phantom shades.

The Winged Spirit (1918)

"My Child Is Dead"

My child is dead—
    Yea—though God has punished,
    I have not sinned,
    Nor wronged a human soul,
    In thought
    Or deed.

My child is dead—
    Aye—and they will bury him;
    Unknowing they will take my life
    And lay it in the tomb
    To be
    Near him.

The Winged Spirit (1918)

My child is dead.
     Oh, show me where the justice, .
     Where the wrong in me!
     Though I have failed
     I'm blind—
     I cannot see.
My child is dead.

The Winged Spirit (1918)

(*Weaving*)

SILENTLY the willow weaves
Its long, slim leaves
Of shining jade, through
Skies of sapphire blue,
    And Spring is here.

(*Drawing*)

Creeping vine and branches trace
Their course and interlace
An eerie grace and sheen
Upon the jewelled screen
    That Summer makes.

The Winged Spirit (1918)

(*Painting*)

Nature's palette is aglow
With rainbow tints that come and go,
Though rich the harvest for her brush—
Gone is the thrush,
      When Autumn wakes.

(*Sculpture*)

A leaden sky is piling high a drift
Of snow which Winter's wind will shift
To serried rows and later mould
And carve in captured cold,
      When dead the year.

The Winged Spirit (1918)

"Daybreak, New York"

BRIDGES which seem to float in mist
Swing across the river:
And spires emerge from out the gloom,
As daylight breaks aslant the city.
Sunlight, catching the golden pinacle
Of the great tower,
Lights a taper for the day;
Then robed in pink,
Creeps down the tower's eastern wall,
To lose itself at last
In mist and city smoke.

The Winged Spirit (1918)

Love is,
Love is here,
Love is there,
Love is everywhere.

Hearts sigh,
Here,
There,
Everywhere.

Hearts cry,
Hearts cry here,
Hearts cry there,
Hearts cry everywhere.

Hearts die,
Here,
There,
Everywhere.

Love lives,
Love lives here,
Love lives there,
Love lives everywhere.

The Winged Spirit (1918)

"Poetry I"

SOMETHING we feel
Yet never touch,
Something that will flee
Swift and sure
From over-much
Pursuing.

Thought, illusive,
Struggling through art
To birth

God's soul
On earth
Moulding man's spirit
From his heart
Of clay.

The Winged Spirit (1918)

THE infant Soul,
Suckling at the breast
Of its mother, Earth,
With wide blue eyes
That stare
Unseeing
Into the wider blue
Of sky,
Not knowing of its birth,
Yet dreaming to its goal.

The Winged Spirit (1918)

"The Universe"

NOTHING in the universe is fixed,
Nor God—nor purpose.

The Winged Spirit (1918)

FROM out the fading beauty of the world
New beauty springs,
As death brings forth
New life.

THE green of Life eternal sleeps
Beneath the Winter snows.

Off-flinging all your covering,
As the Winter goes, you come
Bearing in your arms from sleep
The poppy and the rose.

"Your Name"

How your name sings to me!
Its music echoes down the years,
And I hear it with a sense
Of nearing music,
Heard long ago in dreams.

How the hours sped away that night on wings!
Yet in those magic moments,
When the past and the future are HERE and
    NOW,
Time is timeless,
And the hours vibrate only as the pulse of
    Time.

"In the Studio"

Who kneels in prayer,
Kneels to his own spirit.

"To Be Free"

I AM suffering with that hunger
That first brought life to earth,
Aching with the pain that bears
The burden of the years.

I am faint with a thirst
As ancient as the sea,
And though I am spent
With love and longing,
Yet am I yearning
To be free.

The Winged Spirit (1918)

"Scattered Dreams"

ALTHOUGH my dreams
From day to day
May break and scatter
As spent waves
Upon the shore,
Beyond the moment
Ever lies the hour
When dream and goal
Shall meet.

Past the breaking waves,
Past the rocks and storm,
There lies
The meeting line
Of sky and sea,
Clasped in the quiet
Of eternity.

The Winged Spirit (1918)

HEARTS may die
Many deaths,
Many hearts lie dead.

While there is life,
Love cannot die,
Love knows no death.

The Winged Spirit (1918)

As the sea
Takes her mood
From the sky,
So do I
From you.
The greyness
Of your present mood
Grips me,
And holds me tight,
I feel so near
The night
That comes to you.

The Winged Spirit (1918)

Part III

MARRIAGE

"God"

THE love
I loved you with
Is God.

The Marriage Feast (1920)

"What Mighty Wooing" [excerpt]

When the earth was young
And had but winds for play,
She gave birth to mountains,
And tore from her living heart
Great rivers that the sea might be,
And her imperial pulse
Was the beating of eons' wings
That thundered past her
In her dreams.

And now the creeping pulse of time
Is no deeper than our days and nights,
And men forget to dream.

The Marriage Feast (1920)

IN a night of storm
I was carried on a sea of pain.
Again and yet again it flung me back
Bleeding upon the rocks.
But my spirit would not yield,
And wore a smile upon its lips.

Now at the dawn
I lie within the sanctuary of your arms.
My spirit weeps at last;
It cannot bear the pang of living joy.

The Marriage Feast (1920)

WHAT is it weighs me down to-day,
With a weight that is sweet,
Like the burden gladly borne
For some beloved?

Is it the shadow of your nearness,
The sense of you too near to me,
Which, though it weighs me down,
Yet brings with it some comfort?

The Marriage Feast (1920)

Or is it just the weight of all my lives
I feel oppressing,
In years which I would lift
And throw aside,
To live again that other life
Where I so gladly died
For loving you.

The Marriage Feast (1920)

"Your Touch"

EVEN as in spring, when the ice breaks,
And the river is in flood,
Singing over rocks,
Surging over moss-strewn cliffs
To drop from there in darkling pools,
Where diamonds dance and sparkle in the sun,
And pearls, one by one
Go quivering to and fro,
Even such is the music that I know
In your touch.

The Marriage Feast (1920)

REST with your arm outstretched, my sweet,
That I may rest there too,
And all the hours that you sleep,
I shall be loving you,
And while we rest and sleep, my dear,
God will hold us two.

LOVE which holds back
Something in reserve
Will never know
The joy of giving,
The joy of constant death.

"You Ask Me"

You ask me if I love you,
    And I answer that I do.

You ask me why I love you,
    And I find it hard to say.
    I come to you.
    You answer every need.
    Your love is all the reason
    That my love can give
    For loving you.

The Marriage Feast (1920)

Love you always?
    That I cannot say.
    It rests with you;
    You lead me now,
    You point the way
    And I gladly follow
    While I may.
    Love is an awakening,
    Another birth,
    A closer homing
    To our mother earth,

The Marriage Feast (1920)

"Time"

TIME, Man has found some fallen feathers from
    your wings.
He has named this one an hour, that one a day,
    others years.
Collecting them and counting them he sits,
Towering above them at his play.

So when I catch the flash of sunlight on your
    wings,
And count the years that hours hold
And days that are centuries old
With nothing after,
I hear beyond the walls of space
Your pinioned laughter.

The Marriage Feast (1920)

WHY does my love not see
The empty cup
I am holding up
For him to fill?
Why does he drink of mine
And find good wine
To meet his will,
And still not see
The empty cup
I am holding up
For him to fill?

The Marriage Feast (1920)

"Dawn"

ALL through the years I heard your voice,
And I thought that I should find you
Just beyond the farther hill;

    Yet ever you eluded,
    Seeking the deeper vales.
    The shades grew darker,
    And I lost the way.
    Then when I thought
    The least to find you,
    You were the dawning day.

The Marriage Feast (1920)

NOTHING to say?
With an aching heart, and a fevered brain,
Nothing to say?
With a heart that bleeds of an endless pain,
Nothing to say?
With a world of suffering yet to face,
With a world of love unsung,
Nothing to say?
O God, nothing to say.

FOR months I looked for a sign:
Some word to tell your mood.
And now
By some unknown chance,
I know.

THIS loving may not be unloved,
We are together now;
We two in the hand of God.
We have been alone,
Each in a world
That knows no pity.
This loving may not be unloved.

NAY, Love, why lose our way in words,
Why try to understand the things of earth
Save through the spirit?
Love like ours has given birth
To countless winged thoughts
That draw us each to each.
Nay, Love, what matters speech
With love like this between?
What matters anything to us
Who have this dream?

I MAY not love you
As another would,
For I have lived too fully,
I have understood.
I may not love you
As another would,
For in the heart that I should bring
You'd feel the pulse of every woman
Who has loved
And suffered for her love.
I have lived in each,
Feeling her pain was mine.
I am all these women,
So I may not love you
As another would.

The Marriage Feast (1920)

"In That Ultimate Hour"

In that ultimate hour, Sweet,
When past and future
Meet in you and me,
My spirit reaches out to you
With arms that are outworn,
With unseeing eyes,
With voice long mute,
With lips that ages past
Have done with kissing.
Then, in that ultimate hour, Sweet,
I know why God is silent,
Why God neither sees nor speaks,
Why those unenfolding arms
Have left me free.

The Marriage Feast (1920)

O TAKE my dreams,
And use them—
You who have no dreams—
Take and crush them,
Crush and bruise them,
Like the vinèd fruit;
Make of them your wine.

So shall you drink
And dream,
So shall my dreams be fused,
So shall the purple of my life
Bear fruit.
O take my dreams!

The Marriage Feast (1920)

"Lost"

HEAP flowers on my head.
Now that you have lost me
Crown me with stone,
For this long-loved beauty
Sleeps with the dead.

Heap flowers on my head.
Now that you have lost me
Dream of the lip you kissed,
Dream of the lost beauty
Of the soul you missed.

The Marriage Feast (1920)

Heap flowers on my head,
Now that I am gone.
Now that you have lost me
Crown me with stone.

The Marriage Feast (1920)

Part IV

THE MOTHER

"Woman"

My mother, Earth,
Is plowed
And harrowed
For the sowing.
Like my mother, Earth,
I bear the blossoms,
I do the growing,
I bear the fruit,
The seed
For sowing.

The Marriage Feast (1920)

THIS mother-love is deeper than you know.
Its roots spring from childhood
When I dreamed
Of what a mother's love might be.
It reached the dawn in maidenhood,
And in marriage faced the sun.
And as its flowers blossomed
One by one, its roots went deeper,
And when it learned to weep
And still to keep its sweetness,
I thought the dream complete.

And now comes this storm
To sweep me,
That I may deeper go to seek
And find the truth beyond my dream.

The Marriage Feast (1920)

I AM a woman
And have lived a woman's way
With life.
Now am I big with new life
Soon to have birth.
Take me in your arms
And hold me there,
For the treasure
That I bear
Is rare
And of great worth.

The Marriage Feast (1920)

"Blue"

To-DAY the sky
Is a glorious blue;
I find blue asters too.
O sky, where have you too
Found this magic blue?

You will not tell?
Then shall I ask my little girl
And she will say,
Whose eyes to-day are blue
Where yesterday was gray.

The Marriage Feast (1920)

His eyes are wild and close to nature,
Understanding things unknown,
Things which are in us and beyond us,
All of beauty.

His features are perfect,
Like a young god's;
But it is the look
That startles you
And holds you.

The Marriage Feast (1920)

"To A Son Going To War"

How may I bear this pain?
Must I see you come wounded home,

How may I bear this pain,
I, who have known my heart
To ache and bleed,
And felt my soul quiver
In the very pride of its pain,
That you might come
A conquering god to earth?
Must I, who gave my beauty
For your birth,
Now see that beauty slain?
What man has right to ask
For this—again?

The Marriage Feast (1920)

As death, with grim
Uncertain features hid
In formless night,
Slips in to draw unto himself
The spent and dying year, behold
The light, which from his invisible
Mantle now shines
Upon the new-born year,
Who comes with head erect
    and shining limbs.

The Marriage Feast (1920)

"It Is Not True"

THEY came to tell me in the night
    That you are dead.
    It is not true!—
For flowers grown by you
Still bloom and toss the head.
    It is not true
    That you are dead!

The Marriage Feast (1920)

The birds you loved now wing
Their many-coloured notes
To a coming sun,
Which pours a golden anthem
Out along the spring.
How may this be
    If you are dead?
    It is not true!

You have out-flown the prison cell
We have known you in,
That you might fling
The spirit of your beauty
Out across the world.
    It is not true
    That you are dead!

The Marriage Feast (1920)

"War"

THE hours creep by to-day,
A maimed and crippled throng,
All that are left to speak
Of the winged nights that were,
And dawns that marched
In stately column,
With love triumphant,
And with music.

Now is their tread
The tramp of stumbling feet,
Their song a mumbled prayer.

The Marriage Feast (1920)

These mourning hours, soulless and pale,
Struggling to build each day,
Cry out against the wrong.

The Marriage Feast (1920)

"The Tree"

You have given all your branches to the winds
For harp.
With rooted arms you have held the earth,
And clasped the sunlight
With your leafy hands.
You have watched rain drip
From your green fingertips.
With up-flung head,
With laughter and with song,
You have challenged
All the skies.
You have given birth
To singing shadows.

The Marriage Feast (1920)

I have given all my body to a man
For joy.
My arms have nested babies,
My hand has held my welling breast
To curling infant lips.

Looking down on laughing children
I have watched
For a while
To smile and be at peace,
And never tire
While shadows form and flow . . .
You have gone deeper into things
Than I,
You have gone higher.

The Marriage Feast (1920)

"The Shadow"

Who watch their lengthening shadow
     on the ground
Have turned their faces from the sun.

I was,
I am,
I shall be.
Breasting the sea,
I draw with me
These three—
I was,
I am,
I shall be.

"The Swan"

ALONG the ages
Men have cried
Their gods,
While women followed
With their worship
And their praise.
Now in recent days
One comes and says
"I am His Son."
Men cry again:
He is the One.
But a woman cries:
"He is my son,"
And the miracle is done.

Yet woman knows
Her work undone,
Till man shall claim
The god as son.

The Marriage Feast (1920)

Part V

THE WOMAN

WHY have I
This sturdy strength
Born of the North,
These eyes of steel—
Why these things,
With this sun-warmed
Passion of the South,
This sun-wooed
Quivering mouth—
Why,
When I find
No steel
To challenge mine,
No lips
To cool my drouth?

The Marriage Feast (1920)

"Cat Briars"

THE cat briar leaves
Were caught
By frost,
And turned
To olive gold
And burnished bronze,
The berries
Were nile green.
When they dream
In happier days,
The sun
Gleams through
Green shining leaves,
Of jade
And fruit
Of dusted blue.

The Marriage Feast (1920)

“After Pain”

AFTER all the pain
I wake to-day
To hear my heart
Sing.
It is like
A mountain stream
After rain
In spring,
So full it is
Of fun
And laughter.

THIS rainbow
Is a many-coloured bridge
By which my dreams
May go.

“This Rainbow”

"My Will"

My will is no giant thing;
It is but a child.
Yet its arm girdles a world,
And in its hand are stars.

Each breaking wave
Leaves great bands
Of woven lace
Upon the sands,
Torn and scattered
By the next wave's
Ruthless hands.

"Sea Lace"

HYMN no joy of sleep to me
Who lay long years
Awake beside a sleeping man. . . .

I was brave from day to day,
Wearing my loneliness as a crown;
But when night came
I was again a beggar,
Gnawing at the grief
The sleeping stranger gave.

The Marriage Feast (1920)

I HOPE that none
Will place dead flowers
Above my head
For grace,
When I am dead,
No garland that will fade,
No stone
Disfigured by a name;
Let me wear instead
The glory of the whole
Wide universe
As crown
Above my head.

The Marriage Feast (1920)

You wove a cobweb through the night
Your dream of life and beauty
Hanging by a thread.
So do I seize my right
To draw through my own night
My dream
To hang and gleam
Above my head.

A MAGIC veil
Broods over the earth.
Spring is here,
The time of loving,
And of sowing,
Of birth
And growing.

"Who Am I"

Who am I,
Wanderer in your night,
Who stir your leaves
To murmur in the dark
To stars?

Who am I,
Who lift and peer
Beneath your greenery,
Who listen
As you gleam
And glisten?

The Marriage Feast (1920)

Who am I
But a mood
To rouse you to reveal
Another self—
Wanderer in your night—
   Who am I? . . .
   Who are you?

The Marriage Feast (1920)

"Mirage (Woman to Man)"

I AM lying
With the vast earth
At my back.
It is upholding me.
The lure of the earth
Is in my eyes.
Through me you strive and drive
To reach the earth.
In seeming triumph
And with song,

The Marriage Feast (1920)

Ever you rise to the encounter.
Though you have conquered me,
Age after age,
You have not won the earth.

Though you come on,
Renewing in each age
The ancient struggle to win through,
When your years are spent
I am lying here

With the vast earth
At my back;
I am here
Between the earth and you.

The Marriage Feast (1920)

"Age"

As I pass,
Sometimes in amaze
I stand before my glass
And smile, gazing
Incredulous at the ways
Of youth smiling back at me.
Then look beyond
Where, grim, behind me,
Poised, in silence waiting—
Stands my shadow.
Though I will not see,
I know
My shadow never smiles.

The Marriage Feast (1920)

WHEN I uncaptained go
Out into the night
Let none weep for me,
And let no alien hands
Touch me in my last sleep;
Only the hands of him
Who loved me.
He will remember.

How vast, how empty
Are the reaches
Of this deserted bed.
How lonely;
It is the loneliness of space
I cannot face.
It teaches
Elemental things to me,
Who thought me wise.

"Deserted"

Noт be restless?
Ask the beach not to burn
When the sea has left it;
Ask the tide not to turn;
Tell the day
Not to leave us,
And the night to stay!

My name was so beautiful
  On your lips;
Speak it sometimes
  In the night,
  And I shall hear;
  Whisper to the night
  "My dear."

WITH all my being in my song
There are no gods along the road to fear.
Evil is here where dead men bury dead,
Onward there is no evil way.   Echo
After echo of my song wings on ahead.
The golden gods are calling, I must go.

The Marriage Feast (1920)

Part VI

OTHER WOMEN

"Mary"

I WOULD not paint a young and fair Madonna,
Mother of the infant child.
I would paint the mother of the man,
The woman who has felt pain,
And suffered for her truth;
Who has made a glory of her wrong
Bearing it with courage and with pride;
The one who can smile and keep her faith
When Christ and child have died.

The Marriage Feast (1920)

"When I Am Radiant"

WHEN I am radiant in my joy,
And feel no happiness outstrips my own,
When friends and life conspire
To pour into my lap
Their countless blessings,
And all my heart's a song,
I know that somewhere in the world
A child is dying,
A mother weeps,
New life is struggling
To the light.

The Marriage Feast (1920)

WHAT is the sea?
It is the tears
We women weep
That love may be.

WHILE your wings
Flash the sunlight,
And memory clings
To the quivering touch of wind
That lifted and pursued you
Through the blue,
You do as women do,
You give to life
Your wings.
You give in ecstasy
To unborn things.

THOUGH I am prostrate weeping mother's tears
And feel that there can be no greater loss,
No pain to equal mine,
I know that somewhere else
Are many hearts rejoicing,
Wedding bells are pealing,
A bride trips home,
Somewhere a child is singing,
   Though I weep.

O WOMEN, weep not
For the sons ye bore,
But weep for the great wrong
Done to love
Through War.

"A Farmer's Wife"

I'M alone tonight.
From the sea
The moon has risen
Mellow and full.
As it climbs, the bay steals its colour;
A tree shows against the moonlight,
Where turkeys are roosting for the night.
From the meadow, grazing in silence,
A flock of sheep passes
Like a mass of drifting cloud.
I hear the call of a mallard,
The honking of wild geese
Flying south.
In the house the fire glows,
My candle sputters,
A cricket sings upon the hearth.
My man snores.

The Marriage Feast (1920)

SLOWLY a woman climbs the steps
That lead her to her home.
She drags her feet.
The house looks dead, its windows
Stare empty-eyed into the street,
And from the way the woman walks
I know her eyes give back
The window's stare,
And by the way she turns the handle
Of the door and goes within,
I know the woman's soul
Is not in there.

The Marriage Feast (1920)

HER joy was for a day.
Yet into that day
Were woven tears,
And the sorrow
Of another woman's
Years.

HER love, she said, was deep.
Yet would she weep
To see him share
His joy,
Or find elsewhere.

"The Mill"

IF the mill that grinds the corn should break,
The stream would still run on and women bake

I SAW two faces in a crowd,
One wrapped in fur, over-fed,
Gone soft from indolence,
The other lean, hungry-eyed,
Shivering with bared head.
Neither smiled. . . .
One wore jewels around her neck.
She whose spirit had not died
Bore slumbering jewels in her eyes.

"Two Faces"

SHE ran to meet you.
You were so swift,
So fleet in coming,
She thought your feet
Were winged and sandalled;
You were to her as sunlight
Streaming through an opened door.
She never dreamed
That in your going
You would leave this clay
Upon her garment,
This clay upon her floor.

The Marriage Feast (1920)

I WOULD be off and away,
I would be on the dunes
With the sea and the salt,
With the smell of the kelp,
On my lips, the taste of the spray,
Watching the birds of the sea
Dip to the blue, and soar.
I would weep to the tune
Of the ruthless wave
Swept in from the deep
Of the seamen's grave,
And dance on the shore
To the shade of myself,
Dance in the light of the sun,
Dance as never a one
Has danced—
Weep as never a one has wept.

The Marriage Feast (1920)

For I am the wind
And I am the wave.
I am the earth, the sea and the sun.
For I am the womb and I am the grave,
I the cradle, I the tomb.
I am the joy, the pain.
I have died these things to find;
I have died to live again.

I would be off and away,
I would be on the dunes
With the sea and the salt,
With the smell of the kelp,
On my lips, the taste of the spray.

The Marriage Feast (1920)

"Autumn Mists"

I

Wisps of mist are fingering the bogs.
They seep from the earth,
They creep . . . Silently they creep .
There are no words for mists.

Rhythmus (Jan. 1923)

Autumn Mists

II

Houses ride in the mist,
Fling javelins of flame and light,
Like ships floating
On a silent sea at night.

III

Mist beneath the moon.
On water, blue like steel,
Gaunt trees spy over the stillness
Of the pools, blue like steel,
Mist beneath the moon.

Rhythmus (Jan. 1923)

"Autumn Mists"

IV

Over the winter wheat mist is laid
A thin green veil;
On the marsh the veil is purple,
On water it lies hard
Like a coat of mail.

V

Across the field mist draws in
And wraps the trees,
A shifting mass.
Carved in black they rock,
A herd of elephants
In a sea of dust.

Rhythmus (Jan. 1923)

"Autumn Mists"

VI

I am the mist.
I am the veil of purple and the green,
Light surging from houses in the dark,
The flare of ships at sea,
I the carved woods, heavy, black,
Rocking like elephants in a sea of dust.
I, the image in the pool,
The blue of it . . . like steel.
I am the mist
Veiling my own desire . . .
Smoke severed from the fire.

Rhythmus (Jan. 1923)

"The Desert" [excerpts]

The canyon
Calling . . .

Poetry (Oct. 1924)

Plunged down among hills,
The river
Running . . .

The cry of the river
Sears the night.

Poetry (Oct. 1924)

"The Desert" [excerpts]

Snow fingering far hills,
Capturing lost sunlight
In nets of gold . . .

Blue wind filters down
Through the hills,
Biting the sand.

Poetry (Oct. 1924)

Blue hands of the desert
Reach up.
Stars drip into the night.

"The Desert" [excerpts]

Dusk in the desert—
Shadowless.

Poetry (Oct. 1924)

Night sombre, silent,
Slowly coming over hills
Closer, closer . . .
Pressing dire against you.
Night
Heavy with weight of stars.

Dawn
Staggering with ashen face
Out of the hills.

Poetry (Oct. 1924)

Hooked rugs in the home of Marie T. Garland, New York. Note large kaleidoscopic hooked rug at upper left *Photograph by G. W. Harting.*

THE AUTHOR WITH HOPE, HER DAUGHTER

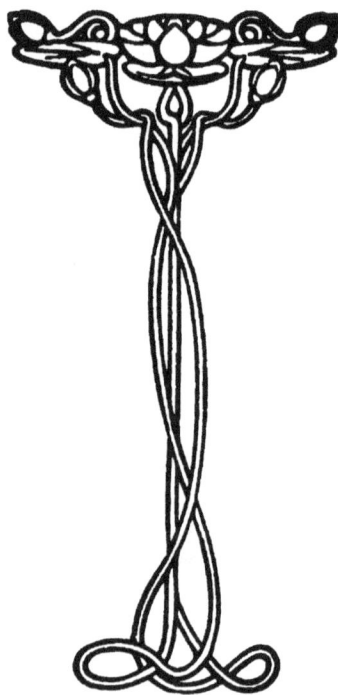

This Space for Your Thoughts

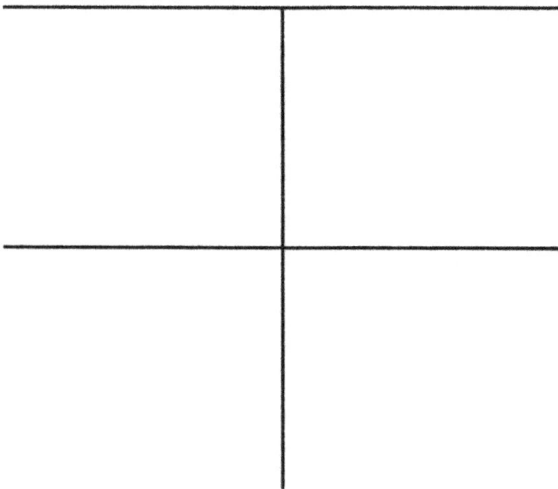

Please handle with care.

www.ingramcontent.com/pod-product-compliance
Lightning Source LLC
LaVergne TN
LVHW041321080426
835513LV00008B/541